Mel Bay's **PRIVATE LESSONS**

Jazz Pentatonics

Advanced Improvising Concepts for Guitar

Online Audio www.melbay.com/20416BCDEB

taught by... **Bruce Saunders**

Audio Contents

1 2 3 4 5 6 7 8 9 0

PENTATONICS ⤳ harmonic applications for the guitar

Pentatonic scales have been explored often and by many authors. It seems, however, that books geared toward the guitar and pentatonics are often concerned with static harmony or vamps. The author writing with the guitar in mind will typically offer the student two pentatonic scales; major and minor. The bulk of the material offered will deal almost exclusively with fingerings, boxes or grids. This particular book is attempting to approach pentatonic scales and their use over more active harmonic movement while addressing the special needs of the typical guitar student. Consequently, it will start with some basic information before addressing some specific uses of pentatonic scales in different harmonic situations. We will briefly explore the use of pentatonic scales and static harmony but the main focus will be to bring the guitar onto the same plane as the piano, saxophone or trumpet and study the relationship of pentatonic scales and chord changes.

This will take a lot of work on the part of the typical guitarist, especially one accustomed to approaching the guitar visually rather than musically. Clearing this visual wall is the first step toward negotiating chord changes with the primary focus a musical one. This is not to say that a grid, grip, box or dots are not helpful tools but that a more complete knowledge of how a specific note relates to harmony and how that note sounds against the underlying harmony is very important.

A lot of practice is necessary to add some of these scales to your repertoire of improvisational colors. Some of the sounds will be familiar to many of you and some may be an acquired taste. *When* to use a specific sound is a musical choice and thus the taste, judgement and art of any particular musician is of prime importance. Time feel, sound, rhythm, space and music are in many ways more important than any particular note or scale. As a safeguard against non-musical considerations our mantra might be: The right note at the right time. The right note at the right time. The right note at the right time.

Table of Contents

chapter one: minor seventh pentatonics

The minor seventh pentatonic scale is one familiar to most guitarists. It consists of five notes: root, ♭3rd, 4th, 5th and ♭7th. If considered the C major pentatonic the notes are: root (C), 2nd (D), 3rd (E), 5th (G) and 6th (A). For simplicities sake we'll consider this the minor seventh pentatonic throughout this book.

Ami7 (or C major) Pentatonic scale

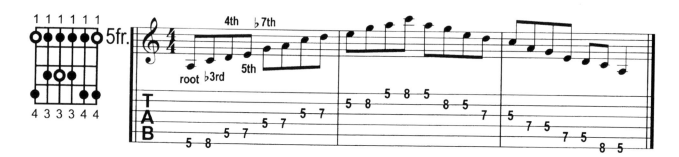

Most guitarists are very familiar with this scale and would use it for a A dominant 7th or A minor chord. Unfortunately, some guitarists can only "see" this scale from the root and if the chord changes, the hand must move to the root of the next chord on the lowest (in pitch) E string. Our first task is to learn some new **perpendicular** (physically up & down) fingerings for the mi7 pentatonic scale. Since the pentatonic is a five-note scale, any one of the pitches in the scale could be part of five other pentatonic scales. Let's use the note "A" as a pivot point.

Pependicular fingerings

The note "A" could be:
Root (Ami7 pentatonic)

♭3rd (F#mi7 pentatonic)

4th (Emi7 pentatonic)

5th (Dmi7 pentatonic)

♭7th (Bmi7 pentatonic)

The Ami7 pentatonic scale located near the fifth fret is at the top of the page. Four other mi7 pentatonic scales in this general location would be:

The note "A" as minor third = F#mi7 pentatonic
F#mi7 pentatonic scale (notice this is the same as A major pentatonic)

The note "A" as fourth = Emi7 pentatonic

The note "A" as fifth = Dmi7 pentatonic

The note "A" as flat seventh = Bmi7 pentatonic

There are other perpendicular pentatonic fingerings available around the fifth fret and you will probably discover these for yourself. It might help to start by knowing the position of each root and visualize the position of the rest of the notes in that particular pentatonic scale. After that, learn the relationship of the rest of the notes in that particular scale to the root of that scale. The ♭3rd, 4th, 5th and ♭7th.

Exercise 1 uses the five previously listed minor seventh pentatonics, perpendicular fingerings, all in the general neighborhood of the fifth fret. The fingering is somewhat arbitrary. Try to identify the notes in each scale by their relationship to the root (♭3rd, 4th, 5th, ♭7 and root).

Ex. 1 ⊃ *Five Perpendicular Fingerings (5th Fret)* → 🅟 *No. 2*

E xercise 2 is the same as Ex. 1 but moved up a minor third. You might try some other locations on the fretboard with this same concept.

Ex. 2 ⟲ *Five Perpendicular Fingerings (8th Fret)* → ⓘ *No. 3*

You might feel somewhat more comfortable with minor seventh pentatonic fingerings if you practiced Ex. 1 & 2 assiduously. But you might have noticed that these patterns don't always flow easily on the guitar fretboard. However, the following **lateral** (physically side-to-side) exercises should sound smooth and fluid if played correctly. You could try sliding down or up to different notes, all down-strokes or anything else to smooth out the line.

Ex. 3 ⮌ *Gmi7 pentatonic lateral pattern* ➔ *No. 4*

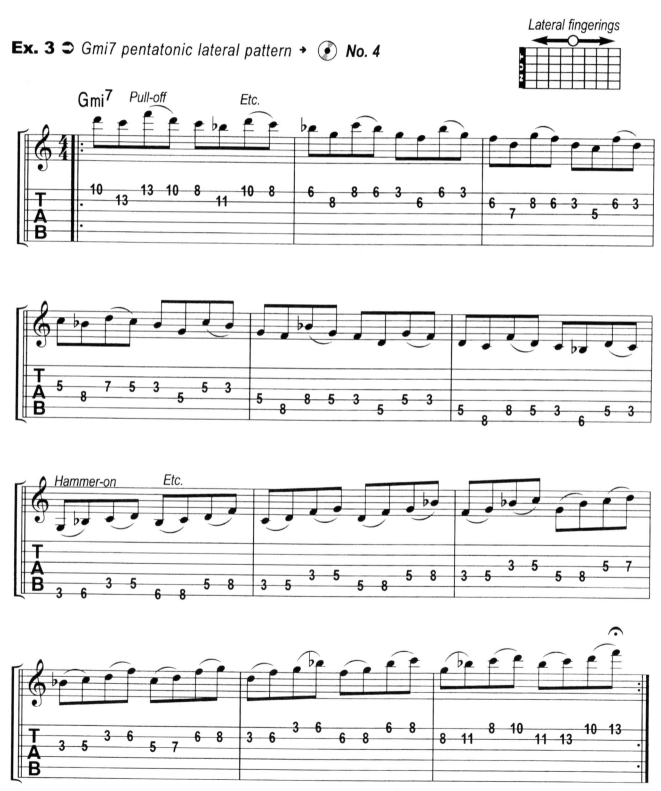

Some variations on the pattern.

Ex. 4 ⭢ *Variation #1 on Gmi7 pentatonic pattern* ➔ 🎵 *No. 5*

Ex. 5 ⭢ *Variation #2 on Gmi7 pentatonic pattern* ➔ 🎵 *No. 6*

Ex. 6 ⊃ *Variation #3 on Gmi7 pentatonic pattern* ➜ 🕭 *No. 7*

That should give you some ideas for smoothing out minor seventh pentatonics. You might like to play these patterns in other keys. But let's get to some specific uses for this scale.

chord	best choice mi7 pentatonics	interval from chord
CMaj7	Ami7, Emi7	⇧ M6th, M3rd
CMaj7#11	Bmi7	⇩ mi2nd
Cmi7	Cmi7, Gmi7, Dmi7	⇨ Root, ⇧ P5th, M2nd
Cmi7♭5	Fmi7	⇧ P4th
C7	Gmi7, Ami7	⇧ P5th, M6th
C7alt	E♭mi7	⇧ mi3rd

Taking the chords one at a time, the relationship of the pentatonics to the chords works this way

Cmaj7 = Ami7 pentatonic
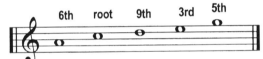

Cmaj7 = Emi7 pentatonic
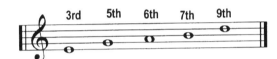

Cmaj7#11 = Bmi7 pentatonic

Cmi7 = Cmi7 pentatonic

Cmi7 = Gmi7 pentatonic
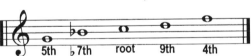

Cmi7 = Dmi7 pentatonic

Cmi7♭5 = Fmi7 pentatonic

C7 = Gmi7 pentatonic
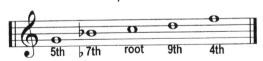

C7 = Ami7 pentatonic
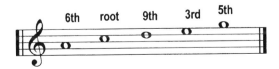

C7alt. = E♭mi7 pentatonic
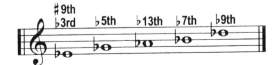

Ex. 7 ⊃ *Patterns over Cmi7 chord (Cmi7, Gmi7, Dmi7 pentatonics)* → 🎧 *No. 8*

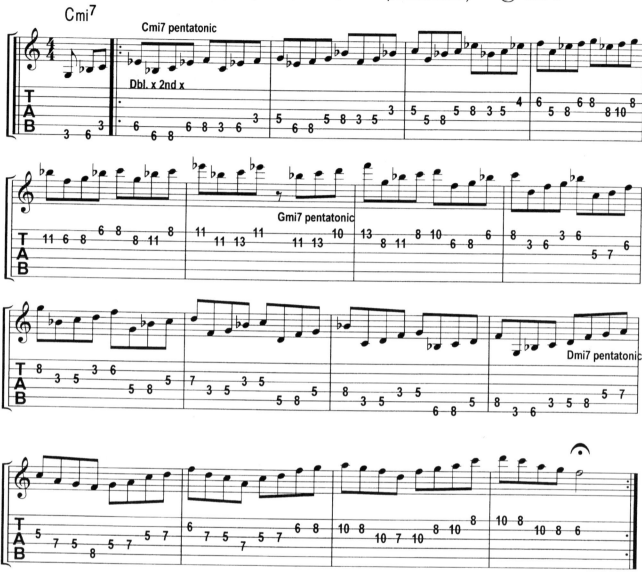

Study No. 1 ⊃ *C minor blues* → 🎧 *No. 9*

CD No. 9 times
:01 Slow
1:05 Fast

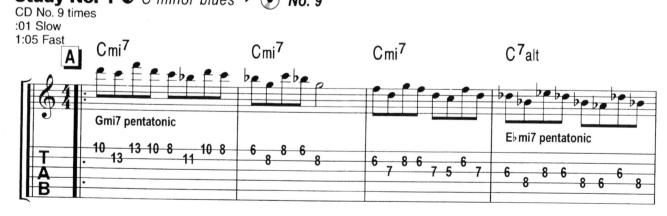

V.S.

Study No. 1 *(continued)*

This next exercise is good for practicing pentatonics on ii-V7-I-VI(7) progressions. Using specific chord/scale combinations the chord qualities get slightly modified. The dominant 7 chords end up as 7alt. chords and the I chord is Maj7(♯11). Please look at the chord/scale combinations below. Notice that the pentatonic scales are moving up by half-steps. See Ex. 10 for practice exercises.

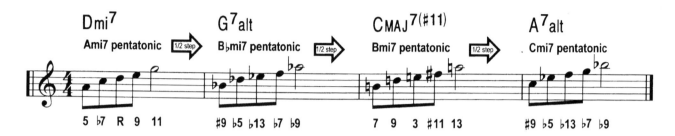

The next exercise is designed to incorporate melodic voice leading by continuing the basic pattern introduced in this chapter through differing scales and chord changes.

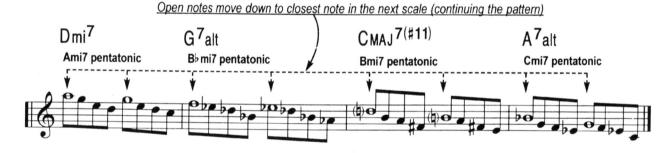

Ex. 8 ⊃ *Ascending half-step mi7 pentatonic using melodic voice leading*

↘ 🞕 *No. 10*

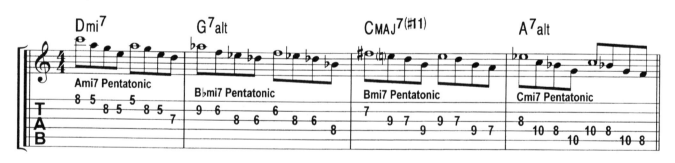

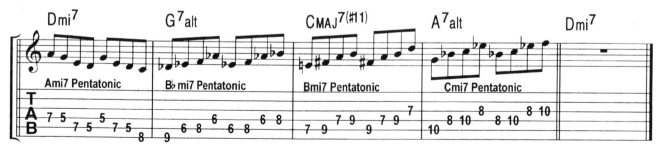

Ex. 9 ⟳ *ii-V-I-VI key of C major, 1/2 step scale movement* → 🔘 *No. 11*

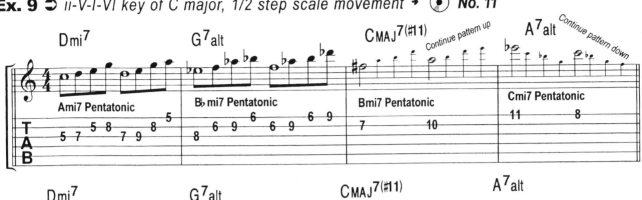

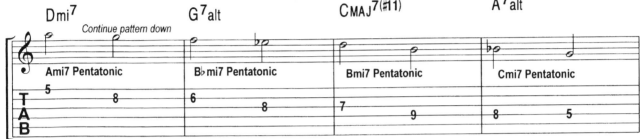

Ex. 10 ⟳ *ii-V-I-VI key of F major, 1/2 step scale movement* → 🔘 *No. 12*

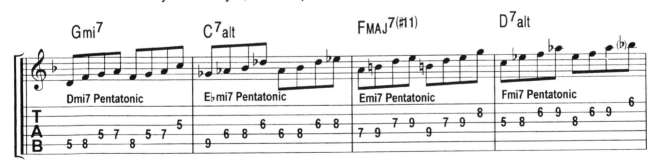

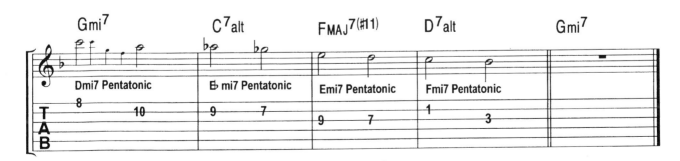

Study No. 2 uses the chord changes to "Autumn Leaves" to explore the sound of the minor seventh pentatonic moving in 1/2 steps on a ii-V-I(MAJ7♯11) progression.

Study No. 2 ⟳ "Autumn Leaves" changes and mi7 pentatonics ✦ 🎵 *No. 13*

CD No. 13 times
:01 Slow
1:34 Fast

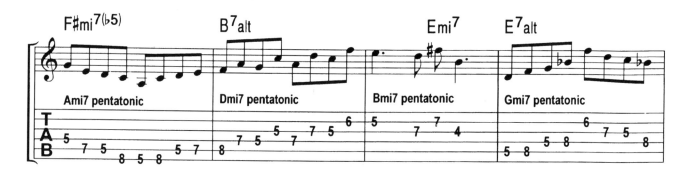

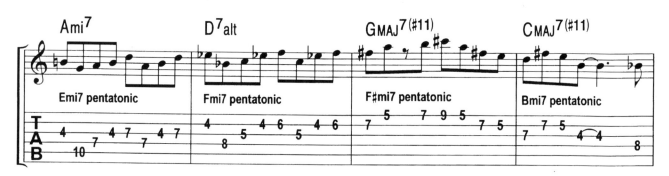

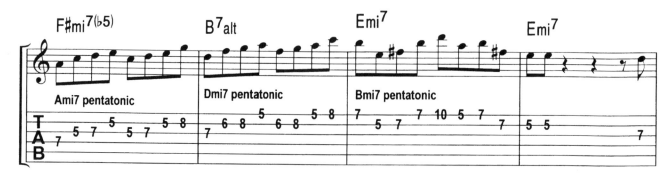

Study No. 2 *continued*

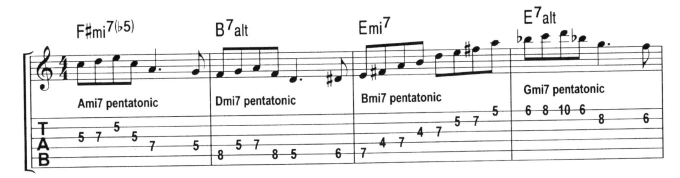

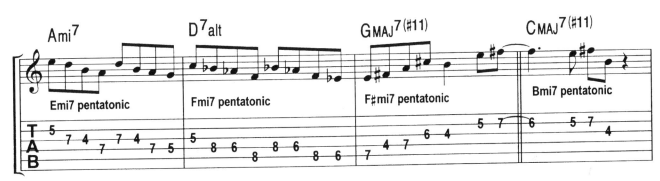

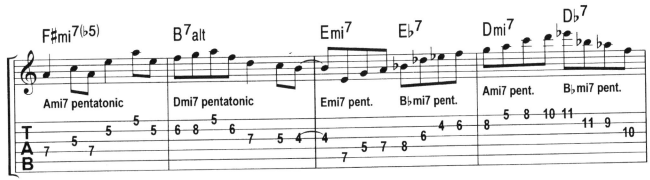

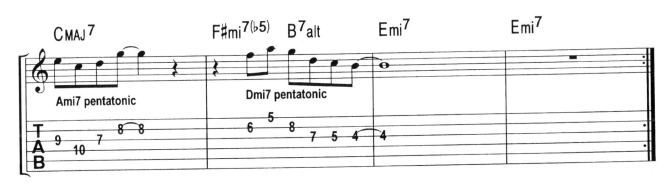

In exercise 11 the idea is to use the half-notes as starting notes for a four-note pattern (up or down by stepwise movement). Use all the fingerings that you have been learning throughout Chapter One. Exercise 12 is minor ii-V-I-(VI) harmonic movement using four-note patterns up and down.

Ex. 11 ⟲ PRACTICE STARTING NOTES *Four-note stepwise patterns* → 🔊 *No. 14*

Ex. 12 ⊃ PRACTICE STARTING NOTES *Four-note stepwise patterns* → (●) *No. 15*

chapter two: minor seventh flat 5 pentatonic

The minor seventh flat 5 pentatonic is exactly that: take a minor seventh pentatonic from Chapter One and flat the fifth. The specific notes are: root, ♭3rd, 4th, ♭5 and ♭7.

Ami7♭5 Pentatonic =

The mi7♭5 pentatonic creates some complicated fingerings due to the major third interval between the ♭5 and ♭7 but leads to some very interesting sounds, as you will soon learn. If you practice the fingerings on the next page you will feel more comfortable with this scale. But first, look at some of the uses of this scale.

chord	mi7♭5 pentatonics	interval from chord	
CMaj7#11	F#mi7(♭5)	⇧	Tritone
Cmi6	Ami7(♭5)	⇧	Maj 6th
Cmi7(♭5)	Cmi7(♭5)	⇨	Root
C7	Emi7(♭5)	⇧	Maj 3rd
C7alt	B♭mi7(♭5)	⇩	Maj 2nd
C7sus♭9 (Phrygian)	Gmi7(♭5)	⇧	Perfect 5th

Cmaj7#11 = F#mi7(♭5) pentatonic

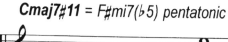

Cmi7♭5 = Cmi7(♭5) pentatonic

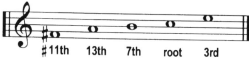

C7alt= B♭mi7(♭5)

Cmi6 = Ami7(♭5) pentatonic

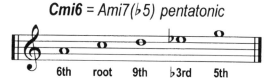

C7= Emi7(♭5) pentatonic

C7sus♭9= Gmi7(♭5)

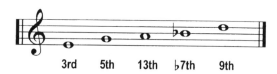

Ex. 13 ⊃ Five perpendicular fingerings *mi7♭5 pentatonic 4th to 8th fret*

→ 🎙 *No. 16*

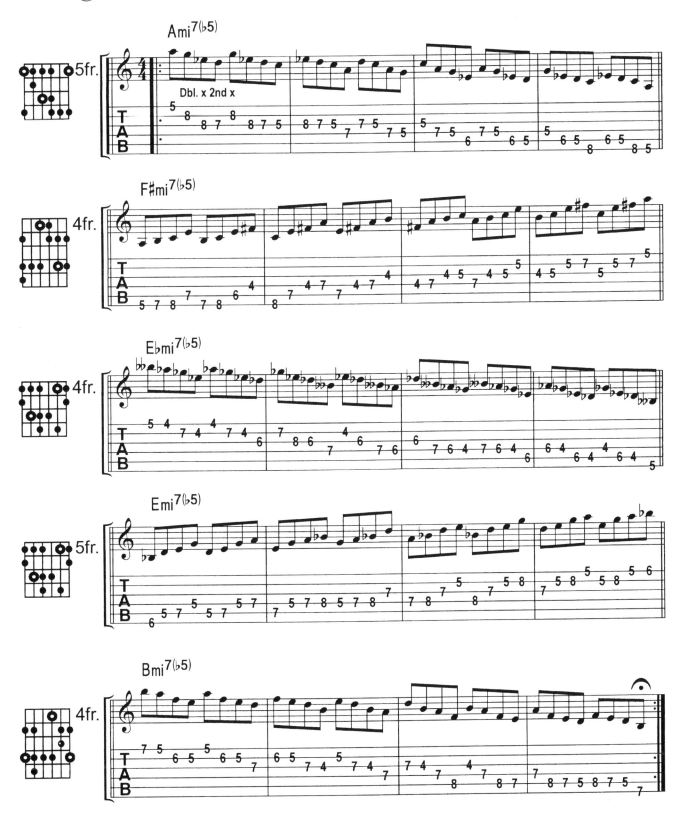

Ex. 14 ↻ Patterns over changes *minor ii-V-i's* → ⊙ No. 17

Ex. 15 ⊃ Minor ii-V-i *with delayed application of new mi7♭5 on V7 chords*

→ 💿 *No. 18*

n Study No. 3 I've tried to again delay the mi7b5 pentatonic used on the V7alt. chord (indicated by [♦]) , a technique we explored briefly on the previous page. You could also try delaying the resolution of the i chord by playing the V7alt. scale into the next measure.

Study No. 3 ➲ *"What Is This Thing Called Love?" changes and mi7b5 pentatonic*

→ 💿 *No. 19*

CD No. 19 times
:01 Slow
1:18 Fast

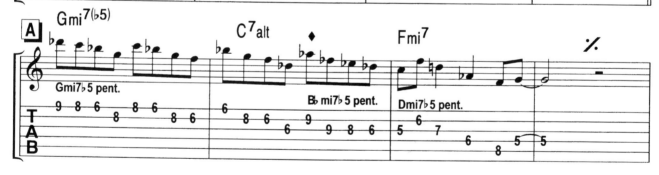

Study No. 3 ↻ *continued*

Ex. 16 ⭕ *Delayed applications* → 🎵 *No. 20*

The 7sus♭9 chord can be confusing. It often functions as something other than a dominant chord. This chord is often notated as 7sus♭9 (eg. C7sus♭9), Phrygian (e.g. C Phryg.) or sometimes as a Maj7♯11 chord over the seventh (e.g. D♭Maj7♯11/C). It is a popular choice for modern jazz composers such as Kenny Wheeler, Richie Beirach, John Abercrombie, John Scofield, et. al. The mi7♭5 pentatonic scale a perfect fifth away sounds nice with this chord.

Ex. 17 ○ 7sus♭9 (Phrygian) → 🎵 No. 21

chapter three: dominant seventh pentatonics

The next pentatonic scale we'll explore is the (major) dominant seventh pentatonic. A variation on the major pentatonic, it's specific notes are: root, 9th (2nd), 3rd (major), 5th and ♭7. (This scale could also be considered the Gmi6 pentatonic). In the key of C those notes would be:

Notice that CMaj7(#11) and C7(#11) use the same pentatonic scale. That is because the scale used this way does not produce a 7th.

Notice that C7alt and Cmi7(♭5) use the same pentatonic scale. That is because the scale used this way does not produce a 3rd.

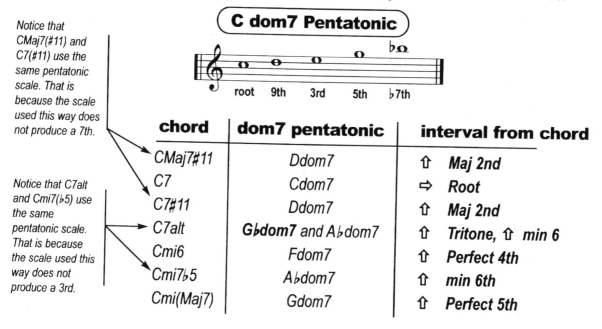

C dom7 Pentatonic

root · 9th · 3rd · 5th · ♭7th

chord	dom7 pentatonic	interval from chord	
CMaj7#11	Ddom7	⇧	Maj 2nd
C7	Cdom7	⇨	Root
C7#11	Ddom7	⇧	Maj 2nd
C7alt	G♭dom7 and A♭dom7	⇧	Tritone, ⇧ min 6
Cmi6	Fdom7	⇧	Perfect 4th
Cmi7♭5	A♭dom7	⇧	min 6th
Cmi(Maj7)	Gdom7	⇧	Perfect 5th

Taking the chords listed above one at a time, the relationship of the pentatonics to the chords is as follows:

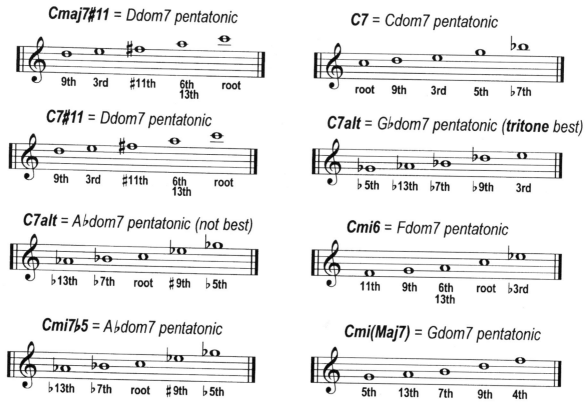

Cmaj7#11 = Ddom7 pentatonic

9th · 3rd · #11th · 6th 13th · root

C7 = Cdom7 pentatonic

root · 9th · 3rd · 5th · ♭7th

C7#11 = Ddom7 pentatonic

9th · 3rd · #11th · 6th 13th · root

C7alt = G♭dom7 pentatonic (tritone best)

♭5th · ♭13th · ♭7th · ♭9th · 3rd

C7alt = A♭dom7 pentatonic (not best)

♭13th · ♭7th · root · #9th · ♭5th

Cmi6 = Fdom7 pentatonic

11th · 9th · 6th 13th · root · ♭3rd

Cmi7♭5 = A♭dom7 pentatonic

♭13th · ♭7th · root · #9th · ♭5th

Cmi(Maj7) = Gdom7 pentatonic

5th · 13th · 7th · 9th · 4th

Check out the sound of this scale on the original studies later in the chapter.

ere is an exercise for the G dominant seventh pentatonic scale. Ex. 17 is a combination of lateral and perpendicular fingerings.

Ex. 18 ⊃ *Gdom7 pentatonic* ✦ ⊙ *No. 22*

FMaj7(#11), G7, F7#11, Db7(b9b13), B7(#9b13), Dmi6, Bmi7(b5) & Cmi(Maj7)

The next two exercises use only dominant seventh pentatonic scales over major and minor ii-V-I progressions. I've used only the tritone application on the alt. dominant chords G7alt.=D♭7 pent.) for it's stronger sound. Another (weaker) choice would be the dom. seventh pentatonic built on the b6. (G7alt.=E♭7 pent.).

Ex. 19 ⮌ *Major ii-V-I sequences* ➜ 🅟 *No. 23*

Ex. 20 ⊃ *Minor ii-V-i sequences* ➜ ⊙ *No. 24*

The following studys use only dominant seventh pentatonic scales, harmonic anticipation (◎), delayed scale application (♦) & resolution to chord tones (⊠).

Study No. 4 ⊃ *F major blues w/ anticipations, delay and chord-tone resolution*

→ ⦿ *No. 25*

Study No. 5 ⊃ *C minor blues (same deal)* → 🎧 *No. 26*

Study No. 6 ⟳ *"Solarize" changes and dom. seventh pentatonic* → No. 27

CD No. 27 times
:01 Slow
:56 Fast

chapter four: major flat 6 pentatonic

This is an interesting and useful pentatonic scale. Again, the name is a description. Take a major penatonic scale 1, 2, 3, 5, 6 (eg. C Major pentatonic = C. D, E, G, A) and flat the sixth (e.g. CMaj♭6 pentatonic = C, D, E, G, A♭).

C Major ♭6 Pentatonic

chord	Major ♭6 Pent.	interval from chord	
CMaj7#5	E Maj♭6	⇧	Maj 3rd
C7#11	D Maj♭6	⇧	Maj 2nd
Cmi(Maj7)	G Maj♭6	⇧	Perfect 5th
Cmi9♭5	B♭Maj♭6	⇩	Maj 2nd
C7#9♭13	A♭Maj♭6	⇧	min 6th

> Remember: the notations above the notes below (such as 3rd, #11, etc.) apply to the key of C. For instance, the first note in the D Maj♭6 scale (D) is the 9th of C7#11.

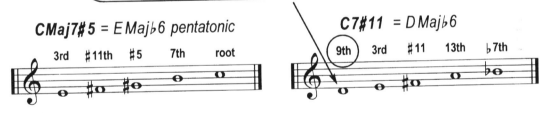

CMaj7#5 = E Maj♭6 pentatonic

C7#11 = D Maj♭6

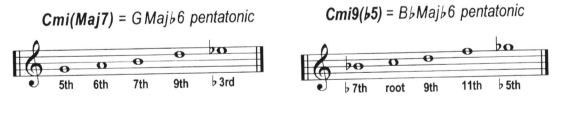

Cmi(Maj7) = G Maj♭6 pentatonic

Cmi9(♭5) = B♭Maj♭6 pentatonic

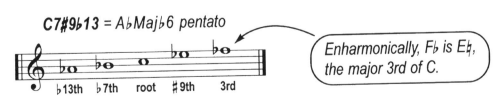

C7#9♭13 = A♭Maj♭6 pentato

> Enharmonically, F♭ is E♮, the major 3rd of C.

The use of this scale can be seen in the original studies later in the chapter.

The use of skips in pentatonic scales can give an interesting sound to an improvised line, especailly in conjunction with a broken rhythmic pattern. We won't be exploring rhythmic concepts in this volume but what follows are some skipping patterns you can study.

Ex. 21 ⊃ *ii-V-i sequence using skips* ➜ 🎧 *No. 28*

Ex. 22 ⊃ *ii-V-i sequence using skips* → ⊙ *No. 29*

Study No. 7 uses only **major ♭6** pentatonic scales but featuring many intervallic skips (leaps). The tab provided is one suggested fingering but may prove awkward or uncomfortable for some. You are urged to explore your own fingerings.

Study No. 7 ⊃ *"What Is This Thing..." changes, skips & major ♭6 pentatonic*
➜ ◉ *No. 30*

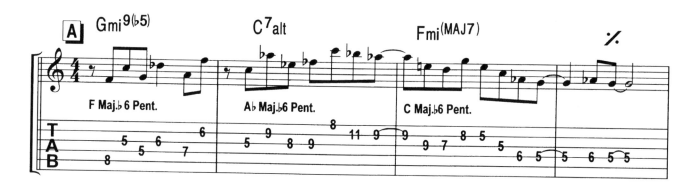

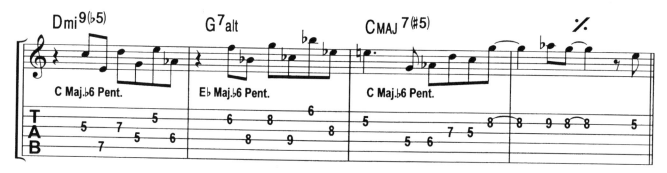

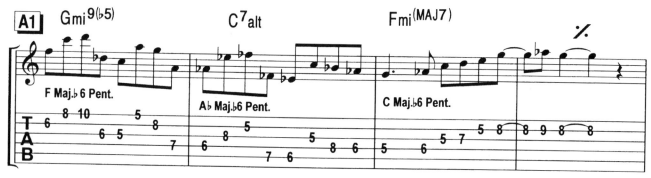

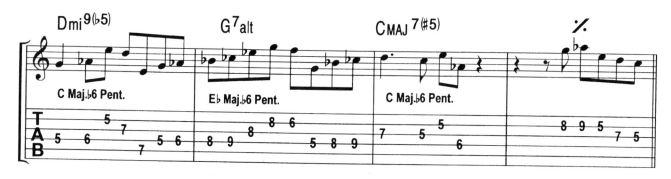

Study No. 7 ↺ *continued*

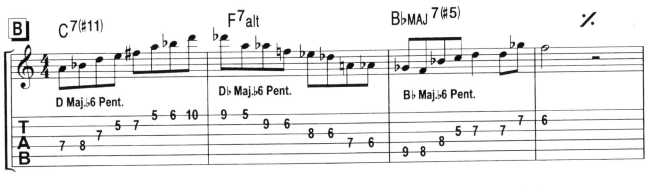

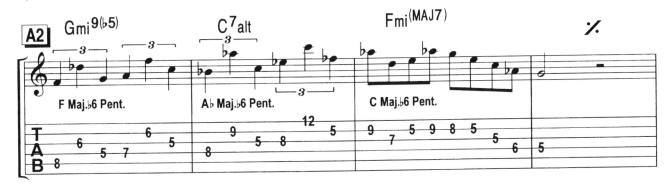

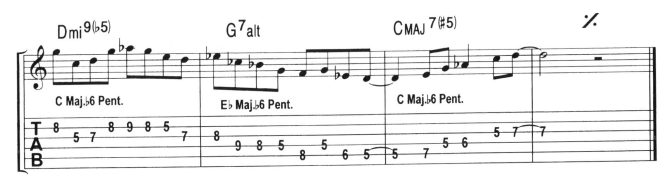

appendix: practice tracks and scale suggestions

hope you've been able to incorporate some of these pentatonic scales into your own playing. I would urge you to listen to players such as Joe Henderson, McCoy Tyner, John Scofield, John Abercrombie, John Coltrane...there are too many improvisors of genius to list here. This appendix provides you with some common chord progressions, some suggestions for pentatonic scales that you might want to try and some answers to questions of previous chapters. Good luck and congratulations for getting this far in the book.

Practice Track # 1 ↪ *"Leaves" changes, key of G, minor 7 pentatonics*
↪ ⊙ *No. 31*

Ami7	D7alt	GMAJ7(#11)	CMAJ7(#11)
Emi7 Pent.	*Fmi7 Pent.*	*F#mi7 Pent.*	*Bmi7 Pent.*

F#mi7(b5)	B7alt	Emi7	E7alt
Ami7 Pent.	*Dmi7 Pent.*	*Bmi7 Pent.*	*Gmi7 Pent.*

Ami7	D7alt	GMAJ7(#11)	CMAJ7(#11)
Emi7 Pent.	*Fmi7 Pent.*	*F#mi7 Pent.*	*Bmi7 Pent.*

F#mi7(b5)	B7alt	Emi7	Emi7
Ami7 Pent.	*Dmi7 Pent.*	*Bmi7 Pent.*	*Bmi7 Pent.*

F#mi7(b5)	B7alt	Emi7	E7alt
Ami7 Pent.	*Dmi7 Pent.*	*Bmi7 Pent.*	*Gmi7 Pent.*

Ami7	D7alt	GMAJ7(#11)	CMAJ7(#11)
Emi7 Pent.	*Fmi7 Pent.*	*F#mi7 Pent.*	*Bmi7 Pent.*

F#mi7(b5)	B7alt	Emi7 Eb7	Dmi7 Db7
Ami7 Pent.	*Dmi7 Pent.*	*Emi7 Pent. Bbmi7 Pent.*	*Ami7 Pent. Bbmi7 Pent.*

CMAJ7	F#mi7(b5) B7alt	Emi7	Emi7
Ami7 Pent.	*Dmi7 Pent.*	*Bmi7 Pent.*	*Bmi7 Pent.*

Practice Track # 2 ↻ *"Leaves" changes, key of B♭, minor 7 pentatonics*

→ 💿 *No. 32*

Practice Track # 3 ⊃ *"Love" changes, key of B♭, mixed pentatonics*
→ ⊚ *No. 33*

A Gmi⁹⁽♭⁵⁾ ... C⁷alt ... Fmi⁷ ... ╱.
F Maj♭6 Pent. ... B♭mi7♭5 Pent. ... Cmi7 Pent.

Dmi⁹⁽♭⁵⁾ ... G⁷alt ... CMAJ⁷⁽♯¹¹⁾ ... ╱.
C Maj♭6 Pent. ... D♭Dom7 Pent. ... Bmi7 Pent.

A Gmi⁹⁽♭⁵⁾ ... C⁷alt ... Fmi⁷ ... ╱.
F Maj♭6 Pent. ... G♭Dom7 Pent. ... Cmi7 Pent.

Dmi⁹⁽♭⁵⁾ ... G⁷alt ... CMAJ⁷⁽♯¹¹⁾ ... ╱.
C Maj♭6 Pent. ... E♭ Maj♭6 Pent. ... G♭mi7♭5 Pent.

B Cmi⁷ ... F⁷alt ... B♭MAJ⁷⁽♯¹¹⁾ ... ╱.
Gmi7 Pent. ... A♭ mi7 Pent. ... Ami7 Pent.

E♭mi⁷ ... A♭⁷ ... Dmi⁷ ... G⁷
B♭mi7 Pent. ... Cmi7♭5 Pent. ... Ami7 Pent. ... Gdom7 Pent.

A2 Gmi⁹⁽♭⁵⁾ ... C⁷alt ... Fmi⁷ ... ╱.
F Maj♭6 Pent. ... B♭mi7♭5 Pent. ... Fmi7 Pent. ... Cmi7 Pent.

Dmi⁹⁽♭⁵⁾ ... G⁷alt ... CMAJ⁷⁽♯¹¹⁾ ... ╱.
C Maj♭6 Pent. ... E♭ Maj♭6 Pent. ... G♭mi7♭5 Pent.

Practice Track # 4 ⊃ *"Solarize" changes, mixed pentatonics*   → 🎵 *No. 34*

A Cmi(MAJ7)   Cmi(MAJ7)   Gmi7   C7alt
4/4 : *Cmaj♭6 Pent.*   *Dmi7 Pent.*   *B♭mi7♭5 Pent.*

FMAJ7(♯11)   FMAJ7(♯11)   Fmi7   B♭7alt
Emi7 Pent.   *Cmi7 Pent.*   *D♭mi7 Pent.*

E♭MAJ7(♯11)   E♭mi7   A♭7alt   D♭MAJ7   Dmi7(♭5)   G7alt
Dmi7 Pent.   *Ddom7 Pent.*   *Fmi7 Pent.*   *Fmi7♭5 Pent.*

B Cmi(MAJ7)   Cmi(MAJ7)   Gmi7   C7alt
Cmaj♭6 Pent.   *Cdom7 Pent.*   *G♭dom7 Pent.*

FMAJ7(♯11)   FMAJ7(♯11)   Fmi7   B♭7alt
Bmi7♭5 Pent.   *Fmi7 Pent.*   *Edom7 Pent.*

E♭MAJ7(♯11)   E♭mi7   A♭7alt   D♭MAJ7   Dmi7(♭5)   G7alt
Dmi7 Pent.   *Ddom7 Pent.*   *Fmi7 Pent.*   *Fmi7♭5 Pent.*

Practice Track # 5 ➲ *Blues in F, mixed pentatonics* ➔ 🎧 *No. 35*

A

F⁷	B♭⁷	F⁷	F⁷alt
F Dom7 Pent.	B♭Dom7 Pent.	F Dom7 Pent.	B Dom7 Pent.

B♭⁷	B♭⁷	F⁷	D⁷alt
B♭Dom7 Pent.		F Dom7 Pent.	Fmi7 Pent.

Gmi⁷	C⁷alt	F⁷	C⁷alt
Dmi7 Pent.	B♭mi7 Pent.	F Dom7 Pent.	G♭dom7 Pent.

B

F⁷	B♭⁷	F⁷	F⁷alt
Ami7♭5 Pent.	Dmi7♭5 Pent.	Ami7♭5 Pent.	E♭mi7♭5 Pent.

B♭⁷	B♭⁷	F⁷	D⁷alt
B♭Dom7 Pent.		Ami7♭5 Pent.	Cmi7♭5 Pent.

Gmi⁷	C⁷alt	F⁷	C⁷alt
Dmi7 Pent.	E♭mi7 Pent.	Ami7♭5 Pent.	G♭dom7 Pent.

Practice Track # 6 ⟳ *"Yesterdaze" changes, mixed pentatonics* → 🎵 *No. 36*

A

Dmi⁷	E♭⁷⁽♯¹¹⁾	Dmi⁷	E♭⁷⁽♯¹¹⁾
Ami7 Pent.	*Fmaj♭6 Pent.*	*Ami7 Pent.*	*Fmaj♭6 Pent.*

Dmi⁷ Dmi⁽ᴹᴬᴶ⁷⁾	Dmi⁷ Dmi⁶	Cmi⁷ F⁷	Bmi⁷ E⁷
Gdom7 Pent.		*Gmi7 Pent.*	*F♯mi7 Pent.*

A⁷⁽♯⁵⁾	D⁷⁽♯¹¹⁾	G⁷	C⁷
E♭dom7 Pent.	*E Maj♭6 Pent.*	*G Dom7 Pent.*	*C Dom7 Pent.*

Cmi⁷ F⁷	B♭ᴹᴬᴶ⁷ E♭ᴹᴬᴶ⁷	Emi⁷⁽♭⁵⁾	A⁷alt
F Dom7 Pent.	*Dmi7 Pent.*	*Emi7♭5 Pent.*	*Gmi7♭5 Pent.*

B

Dmi⁷	E♭⁷⁽♯¹¹⁾	Dmi⁷	E♭⁷⁽♯¹¹⁾
Ami7 Pent.	*B♭mi7 Pent.*	*Ami7 Pent.*	*B♭mi7 Pent.*

Dmi⁷ Dmi⁽ᴹᴬᴶ⁷⁾	Dmi⁷ Dmi⁶	Cmi⁷ F⁷	Bmi⁷ E⁷
Gdom7 Pent.		*Gmi7 Pent.*	*F♯mi7 Pent.*

A⁷⁽♯⁵⁾	D⁷⁽♯¹¹⁾	G⁷	C⁷
E♭dom7 Pent.	*E Maj♭6 Pent.*	*G Dom7 Pent.*	*C Dom7 Pent.*

Cmi⁷ F⁷	B♭ᴹᴬᴶ⁷ E♭ᴹᴬᴶ⁷	Emi⁷⁽♭⁵⁾	A⁷alt
F Dom7 Pent.	*Dmi7 Pent.*	*Emi7♭5 Pent.*	*Gmi7♭5 Pent.*

Answer Key pg. 18 ⟳ *Minor seventh pentatonics patterns* ♦ ⊚ *No. 14*

Answer Key pg. 19 ⊃ *Minor seventh pentatonics patterns* → ⓟ *No. 15*

BRUCE SAUNDERS

Bruce Saunders has been working in the New York jazz community since 1987. A native of Florida, Bruce earned his masters degree in jazz performance from North Texas State University and soon after, moved to New York city. While at North Texas on scholarship, Bruce received additional scholarships from the Dallas Jazz Society and played in the One O'clock Lab Band, with whom he made 3 recordings.

Since arriving in New York, he has gone on to record with: Jack DeJohnette, Peter Erskine, Dave Holland, Kenny Werner, Bill Stewart, Dave Pietro, Michael Cain, Glen Velez and many others. He has performed with: Bobby Previte, Scott Colley, George Garzone, Hal Crook, Guy Klucevek, Ray Anderson, and many others. He has toured Europe, South America, Australia, Japan and the United States.

Bruce's first CD as a leader ("Forget Everything") was released in 1996 and featured Jack Dejohnette on drums, Michael Cain on piano, Dave Pietro on saxophone and Tony Scherr on bass. His 2nd CD "Likely Story" (Moo Records) was released in the United States in the fall of 1999 (released Japan 1998) and includes Peter Erskine (drums), Otmaro Ruiz (piano), Dave Carpenter (bass) and Dave Pietro, esq.

In addition to his playing career in New York, he has been active in the teaching community as well. Since 1989 Bruce has been on the faculty of the Berklee School of Music (Boston) where he leads classes in improvisation, jazz harmony, ensembles, and teaches private guitar lessons. He performs often at Berklee with other faculty members, playing at least 1 concert each semester.